T0148599

Scales & Chords
for the
Beginner Pianist

STEPHEN VAN DER HOEK

BALBOA.PRESS
A DIVISION OF HAY HOUSE

Balboa Press books may be ordered through booksellers or by contacting:

Balboa Press
A Division of Hay House
1663 Liberty Drive
Bloomington, IN 47403
www.balboapress.com.au
1 (877) 407-4847

Because of the dynamic nature of the Internet, any web addresses or links contained in this book may have changed since publication and may no longer be valid. The views expressed in this work are solely those of the author and do not necessarily reflect the views of the publisher, and the publisher hereby disclaims any responsibility for them.

The author of this book does not dispense medical advice or prescribe the use of any technique as a form of treatment for physical, emotional, or medical problems without the advice of a physician, either directly or indirectly. The intent of the author is only to offer information of a general nature to help you in your quest for emotional and spiritual well-being. In the event you use any of the information in this book for yourself, which is your constitutional right, the author and the publisher assume no responsibility for your actions.

Any people depicted in stock imagery provided by Getty Images are models,
and such images are being used for illustrative purposes only.
Certain stock imagery © Getty Images.

ISBN: 978-1-5043-2158-7 (sc)
ISBN: 978-1-5043-2163-1 (e)

Print information available on the last page.

Balboa Press rev. date: 05/14/2020

For my students at
Torrens Valley Christian School

Contents

Introduction

I never imagined earlier in my life that I would be publishing a book such as this. However, as I found myself teaching beginners the piano, a book of scales and chords that I liked became difficult to find. So, as they say, "When you want something done properly, do it yourself!"

The idea for this book came about from using *The Russian School of Piano Playing*, Book 1, Part I[1]. I have found this book to be a solid and reliable introduction to the piano for all ages, and despite its simplicity in design and lack of gimmicks, has never disappointed me or my students in providing interest and a steady line of progress. In the back of that volume, the authors write:

> During the first stage of learning scales (approximately from the second half of the first year of study), the pupil can learn several major scales in two octaves direct and contrary motion and one or two minor scales (melodic and harmonic) in keys he knows from pieces. Scales should be studied in an order of ascending fifths, starting with C. All scales should be played initially hands separately, first one octave, then two. When starting to play scales hands together, the first scales are best played in contrary motion (starting from the same note) as the fingers are then symmetrically disposed on the keyboard, and only later in parallel motion (p 40).

I have sought to follow this paedagogical scheme, and to provide a more expanded form of the material provided in the back of that book (with the exception of including melodic minor scales, which I have included in an appendix should anyone wants to use them). Therefore, in my own teaching, this book forms somewhat of a companion volume to the Russian book, but could also be used by itself with other resources. Like the Russian book, the written text provided is more for the teacher's benefit, than for the student's (depending on age).

---

[1] *The Russian School of Piano Playing*, Book 1, Part I, compiled by E. Kissell, V. Natanson, A. Nikolaev and N. Sretenskaya, General Editor A. Nikolaev, tr Narineh Harutyunyan & Martin Hughes, Boosey & Hawkes: 1978.

I cannot emphasise highly enough how important the study of scales, chords and arpeggios is in forming young pianists. It is not sufficient that students simply absorb these skills through repertoire alone, as if a solely repertoire-based study implies a more "fun" or "leisurely" approach. So often, there are too many students who don't study finger technique or sight-reading, such that they become too dependent on the teacher. Many amateur students of the piano do not have the skills to play at all for fun or leisure, because they were never taught to read music properly, or grounded in technique. They sometimes end up having almost nothing to show for many years of lessons.

It is easy enough to find various charts of scales and arpeggios, but many of them I found to appear either too lofty for the beginner, or too facile. I wanted to have a book that looked inviting, and gave beginners the assistance they need, while at the same, gave ample scope for the student's improvement and development.

Particular features of this book are the use of unfilled note-heads to indicate the white notes on the piano, and filled note-heads to indicate the black notes. Also, the beaming of the notes indicates hand positions. These features should provide some visual assistance to students beginning to learn their scales, and serve as an aid for memorisation.

Also, I have attempted to provide assistance in "building the scale" by breaking the scale into hand positions, to give students a step-by-step process, enabling them to learn the musical elements with confidence and achieve the finished product without too much frustration.

I commend this volume to teachers and students alike, and I hope it can be of some use.

Stephen van der Hoek
March 2020

Scales

RIGHT HAND

Building the Scale

First, we play the first hand position, starting on C.

Next, we play the second hand position, starting on F.

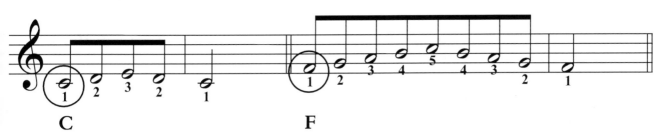

Next, we practice joining the two hand positions together, by crossing the thumb under the 3rd finger.

Now, we practice starting from the top of the scale, and crossing the 3rd finger over the top of the thumb.

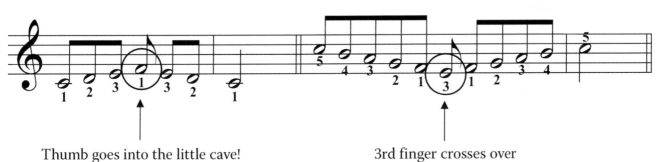

Thumb goes into the little cave!

3rd finger crosses over

Now, we join the whole scale together, crossing the thumb under on the way up, and crossing the 3rd finger over on the way down.

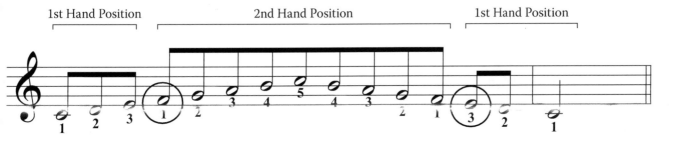

You can start a scale on any note on the piano. The scale we are leagning now is called a "C major scale", because it starts on C. We can sing the letter names of the notes like this:

C D E F G A B C B A G F E D C

You can also name the notes with the "Sol-fa" names. You might know these names from the movie, "The Sound of Music".

Do Re Mi Fa So La Ti Do Ti La So Fa Mi Re Do

When we begin a scale on a different note, the letter names of the notes change. But the "Sol-fa" names stay the name. For example, here is a major scale starting on G (a "G major scale").

G   A   B   C   D   E   F# G   F# E   D   C   B   A   G
Do Re Mi Fa So La Ti Do Ti La So Fa Mi Re Do

Can you see? In C major, Do is on C, but in G major, Do is on G.

Stephen van der Hoek

C major

G major

G major has an F♯.

D major

D major has two sharps: F♯ and C♯.

A major

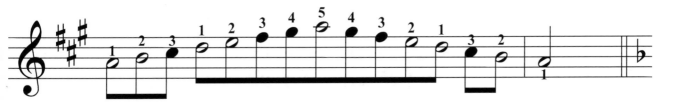

F major

F major has an B♭.

Notice the different fingering!

A minor

A minor has a raised seventh: G♯.

E minor

E minor has a sharp in the key signature (F♯), and a raised seventh (D♯).

D minor

D minor has a flat in the key signature (B♭), and a raised seventh (C♯).

Stephen van der Hoek

LEFT HAND

Building the Scale

Left hand scales are similar to the right hand one, except the fingering is upside-down.

First, we play the first hand position, starting on C.

Next, we play the second hand position, starting on A.

C

A

Next, we practice joining the two hand positions together, by crossing the 3rd finger over the top of the thumb.

Now, we start at the top of the scale, and cross the thumb under the 3rd finger.

Third finger crosses over

Thumb goes into the little cave!

Now, we join the whole scale together, crossing the third finger over on the way up, and crossing the thumb under on the way down.

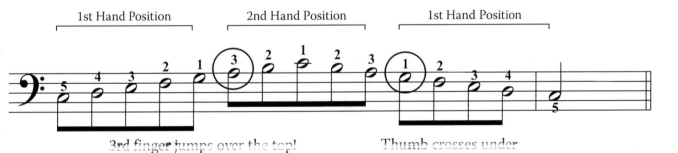

3rd finger jumps over the top!

Thumb crosses under

C Major

G Major

D Major

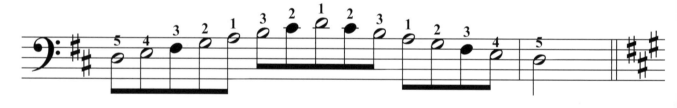

A Major

Stephen van der Hoek

F Major

A Minor

E Minor

D Minor

Two Octaves

RIGHT HAND

Building the Scale

When we play a scale in two octaves, we have four hand positions:

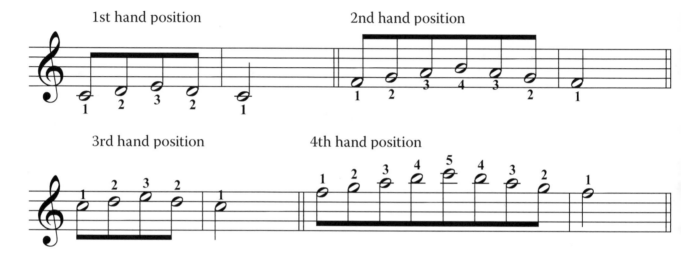

Now, we practice playing a normal C major scale with one octave, but instead of using the 5th finger at the top, we cross the thumb under the 4th finger, which connects to the second octave.

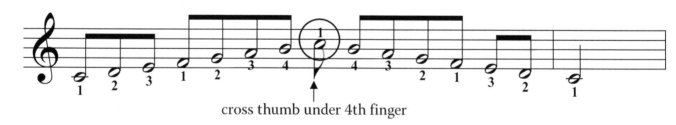

cross thumb under 4th finger

Next, we practice the scale from the top, crossing the 4th finger over the thumb:

fourth finger crosses over

Stephen van der Hoek

Now, we join the two octaves together, crossing the thumb under the 4th finger on the way up, and crossing the 4th finger over the thumb on the way down.

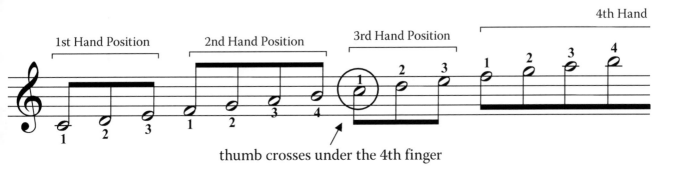

thumb crosses under the 4th finger

4th finger crosses over the thumb

When we play a scale with more than one octave, the thumb crosses under the 3rd and 4th fingers alternately. On the way down, the 3rd and 4th fingers cross alternately over the thumb.

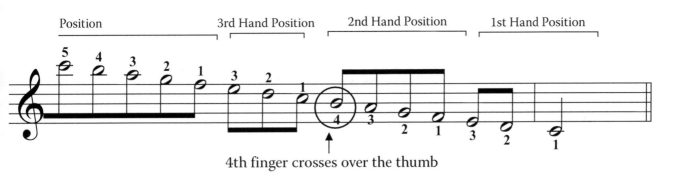

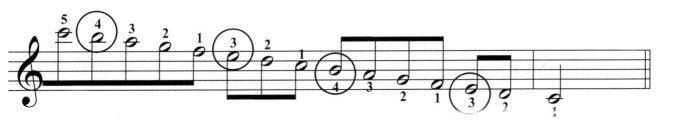

C major

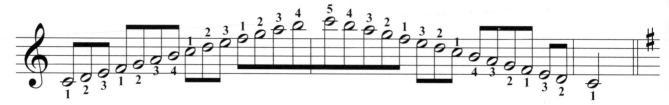

G major

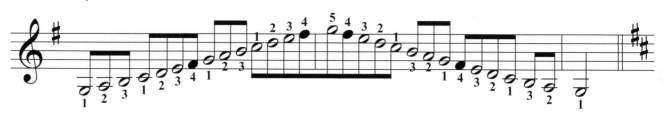

D major

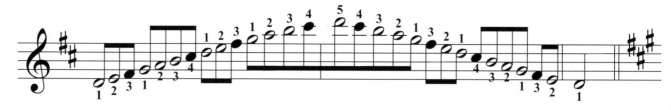

A major

Stephen van der Hoek

F major

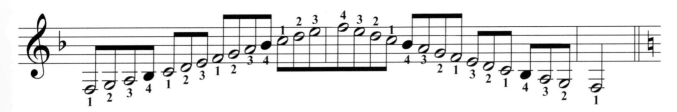

Remember the different fingering for F major.

A minor

E minor

D minor

LEFT HAND

Building the Scale

When we play a scale in two octaves in the left hand, we also have four hand positions:

1st hand position   2nd hand position

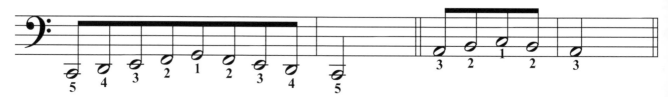

3rd hand position   4th hand position

Now, we practice playing a normal C major scale with one octave, but we cross the 4th finger over the thumb, which connects to the second octave.

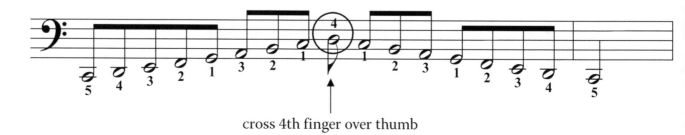

cross 4th finger over thumb

Next, we practice the scale from the top, crossing the thumb under the 4th finger.

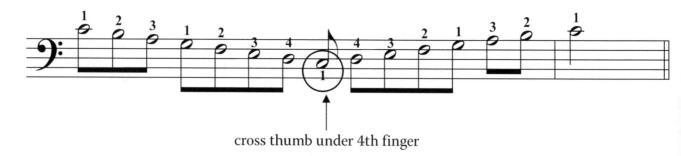

cross thumb under 4th finger

Stephen van der Hoek

Now, we join the two octaves together, crossing the 4th finger over the thumb on the way up, and crossing thumb under the 4th finger on the way down.

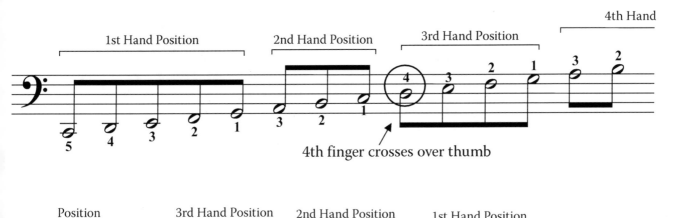

4th finger crosses over thumb

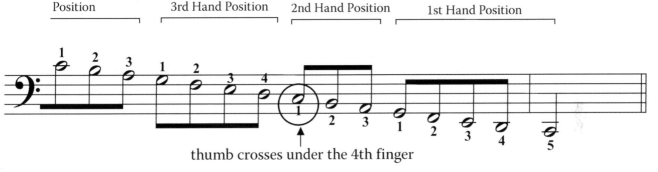

thumb crosses under the 4th finger

When we play a scale with more than one octave in the left hand, the third and fourth finger cross alternatively over the thumb. On the way down, the thumb crosses under alternatively, under the the 3rd finger, and under the 4th fingers.

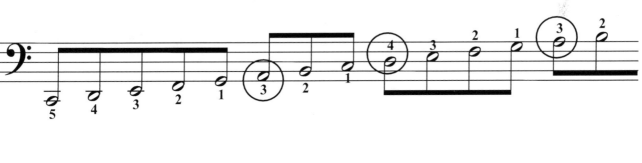

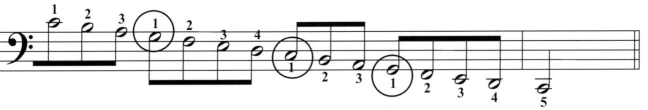

C major

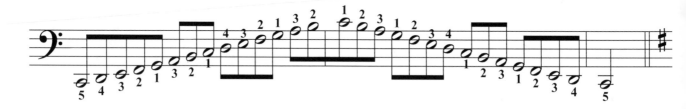

G major

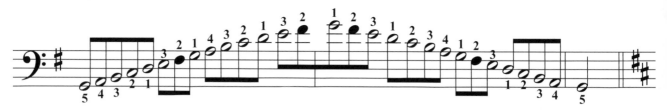

D major

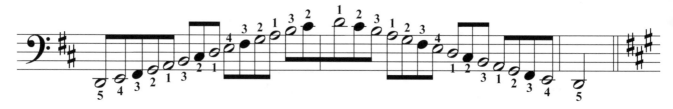

A major

Stephen van der Hoek

F major

A minor

E minor

D minor

Hands Together

Building the Scale

First, we are going to learn how to play the scale with hands together, in **contrary motion**. Contrary motion means that the two hands play the scale in opposite directions.

First, we play the first hand position, hands together, starting with both thumbs on "Middle C". Notice that both hands have the same fingering.

Now, we play the second hand position, hands together, starting on the outer Cs, and moving into the middle. Both hands have the same fingering here too.

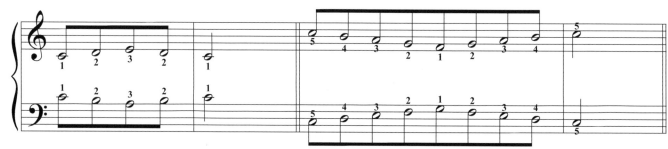

Now we practise joining the two parts together, by crossing the two thumbs under the two 3rd fingers.

Then we start at the outer ends of the scale, and cross the 3rd fingers over the two thumbs.

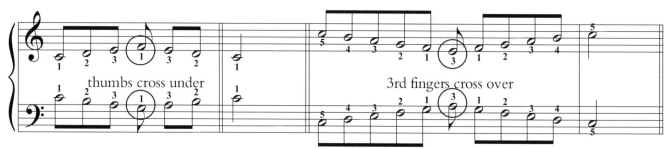

Now, we join the whole scale together in both hands, crossing the thumbs under the 3rd fingers when moving outwards, and crossing the 3rd fingers over the thumbs when moving inwards.

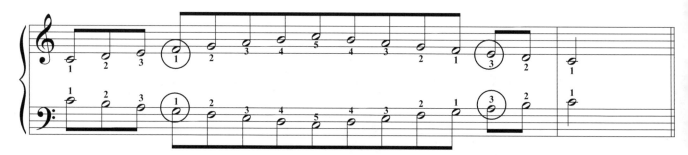

We can also try playing two octaves, by crossing the thumbs under the 3rd and 4th fingers alternatively on the way outward, and crossing the 3rd and 4th fingers alternatively over the thumbs on the way inward.

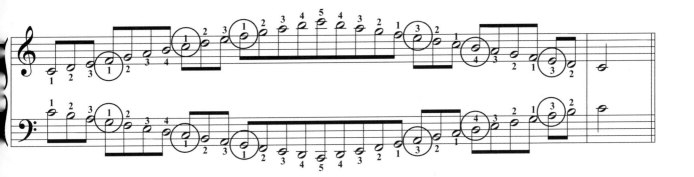

Now, we are going to learn how to play the scale with hands together, in **similar motion**. Similar motion means that the two hands play the scale in the same direction.

When we play similar motion, the two hands have different fingerings from each other, and play different hand positions at different times. This means that the thumbs, 3rd and 4th fingers cross at different times too. However, in C major, the 3rd fingers meet up at the same time.

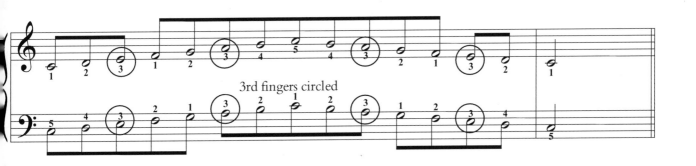

3rd fingers circled

Let's play the C major scale again, but this time, take notice of where the thumbs cross under and where the 3rd fingers cross over.

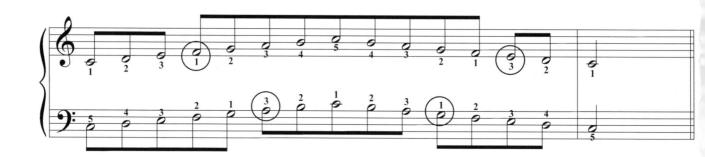

Do you think you can play two octaves? When we connect the octaves together, the thumbs also meet on the note C.

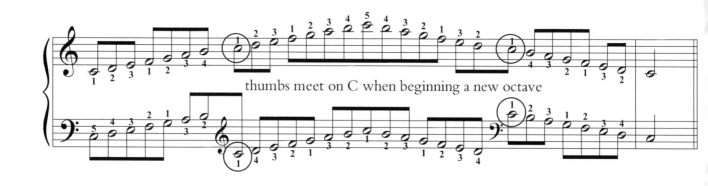

thumbs meet on C when beginning a new octave

Stephen van der Hoek

C major

Contrary Motion: One Octave

Contrary Motion: Two Octaves

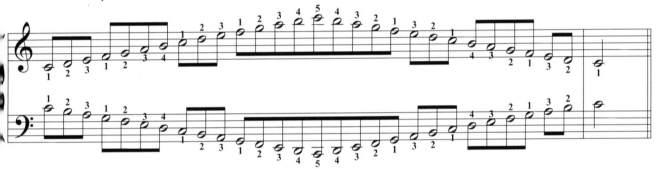

Similar Motion: One Octave

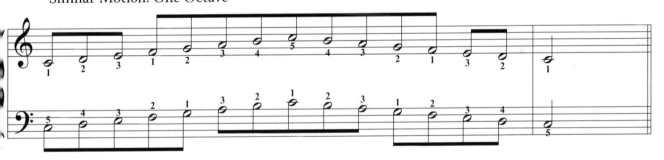

Similar Motion: Two Octaves

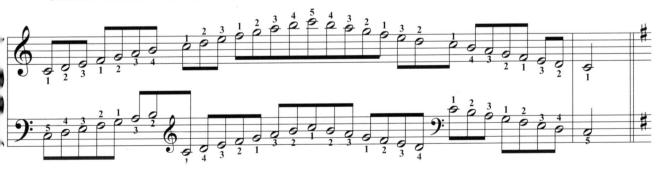

G major

Contrary Motion: One Octave

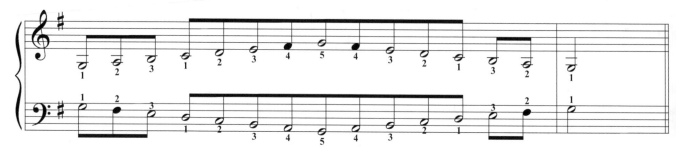

Contrary Motion: Two Octaves

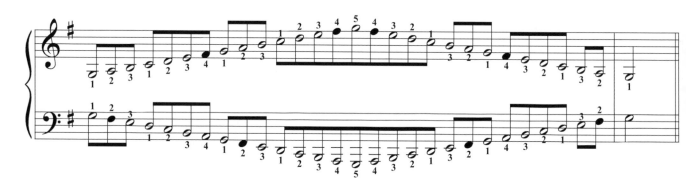

Similar Motion: One Octave

Similar Motion: Two Octaves

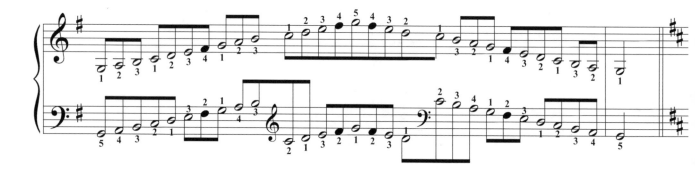

Stephen van der Hoek

D major

Contrary Motion: One Octave

Contrary Motion: Two Octaves

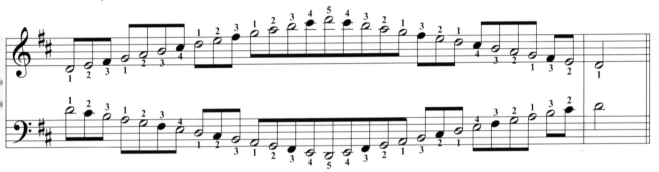

Similar Motion: One Octave

Similar Motion: Two Octaves

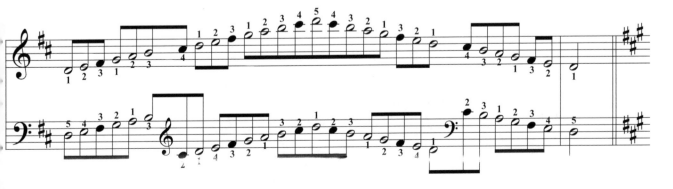

A major

Contrary Motion: One Octave

Contrary Motion: Two Octaves

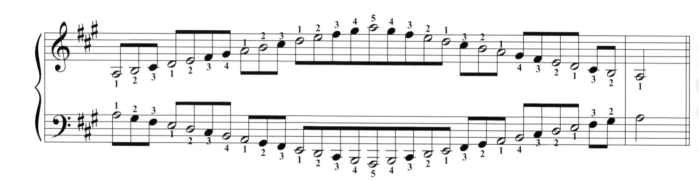

Similar Motion: One Octave

Similar Motion: Two Octaves

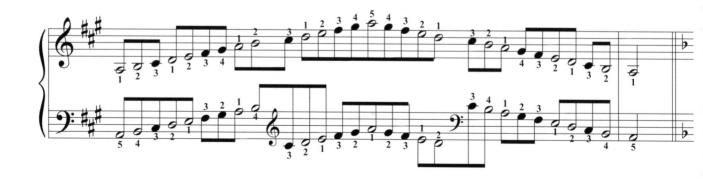

Stephen van der Hoek

F major

Contrary Motion: One Octave

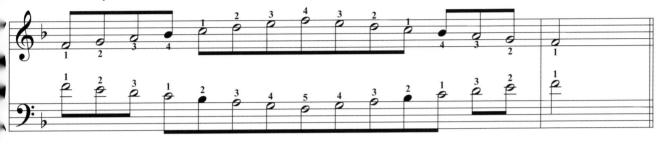

Contrary Motion: Two Octaves

Similar Motion: One Octave

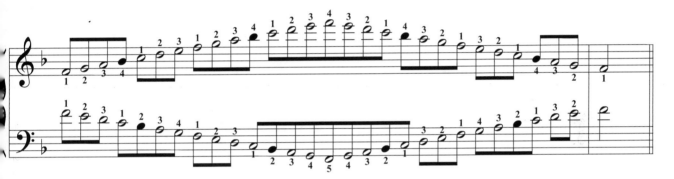

Similar Motion: Two Octaves

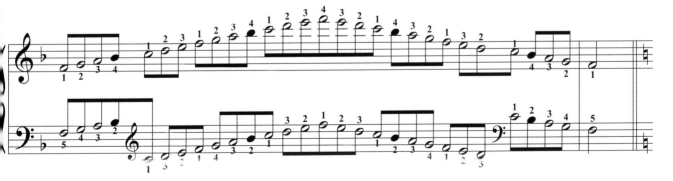

A minor

Contrary Motion: One Octave

Contrary Motion: Two Octaves

Similar Motion: One Octave

Similar Motion: Two Octaves

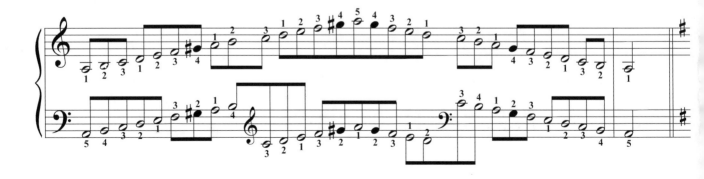

C minor

Contrary Motion: One Octave

Contrary Motion: Two Octaves

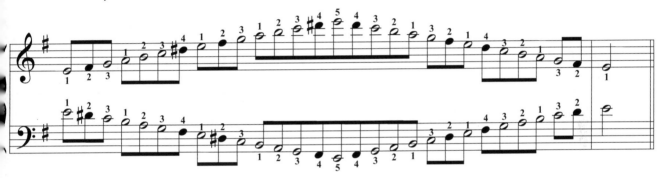

Contrary Motion: Two Octaves

Similar Motion: Two Octaves

D minor

Contrary Motion: One Octave

Contrary Motion: Two Octaves

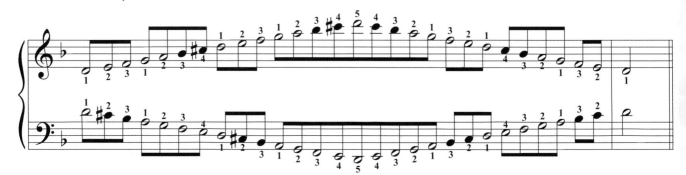

Contrary Motion: Two Octaves

Similar Motion: Two Octaves

Chords

Building the Scale

Just as in each major and minor key, we can play a scale, so also in each key, we can play chords. Scales form the basis of melodies (or "tunes", the part of a piece of music to which we can sing along), and chords form the basis of harmony (the part of a piece of music which accompanies the melody). For example, we might imagine a singer and a guitar: the singer sings a melody (which is made up of parts of the scale), and a guitar plays the accompaniment (which is made up of chords and chord patterns).

A basic three note chord is called a triad. Here's how we build a triad in C major:

First, we play the C, which is called the "tonic".

Then, we play the E, a third higher than C, which is called the "mediant".

Next, we play the G, a fifth higher than C, which is called the "dominant".

Now, we play all three notes together to form the triad.

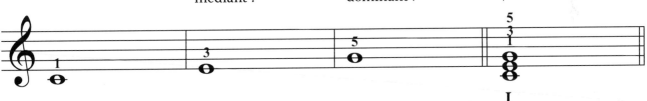

The major chord which is built on the tonic is called **root position**. The "root" note is the note after which the key is named. For example, in C major, the root note is C. This triad is called "root position", because the bottom note of the chord is "C" (the root).

We label a triad in root position with a Roman numeral, I (number "1").

Inversions

The word "inversion" mean something turned upside-down. We can take the C major triad, and we can turn it upside-down by putting the notes in a different order to make what we call "inversions". The C major triad has two inversions, which we call "First Inversion" and "Second Inversion".

We build a first inversion chord in the same way as the root position, but we start on the E (the mediant), instead of the C (the tonic).

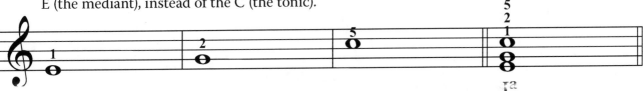

We label a triad in first inversion with a Roman numeral "I", and a letter "a".

We build a second inversion chord in the same way as the root position and first inversion, but we start on the G (the dominant).

Iᵇ

We label a triad in first inversion with a Roman numeral "I", and a letter "b".

We can play the triads next to each other, in root position, first inversion, second inversion, and again in root position, like this:

And in the left hand like this:

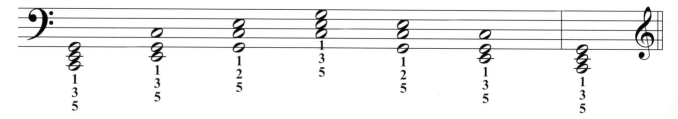

We can also break up the chords into groups of 3 like this (called "broken chords"):

We can also play broken chords in groups of 4 like this:

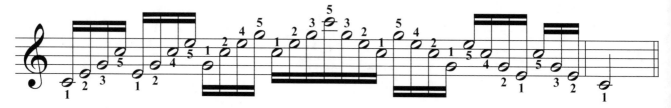

C major

Triads

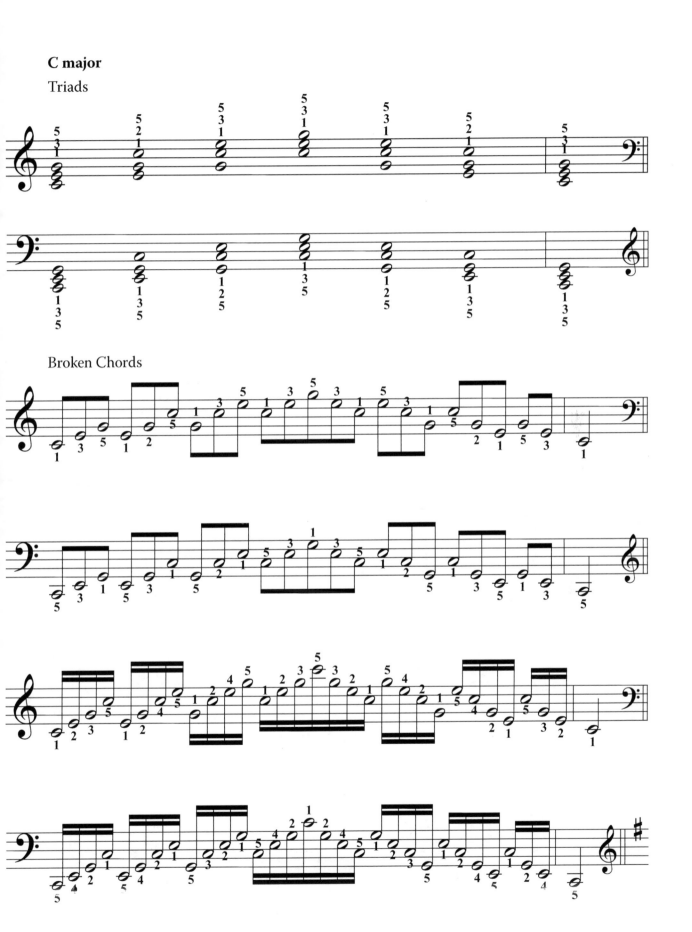

Broken Chords

G major

Triads

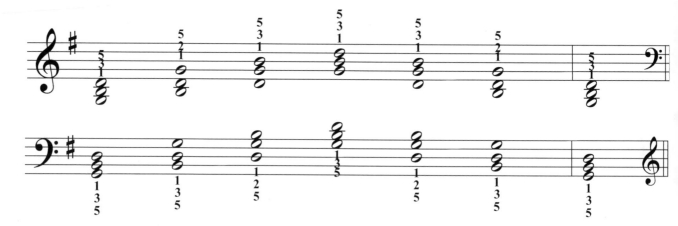

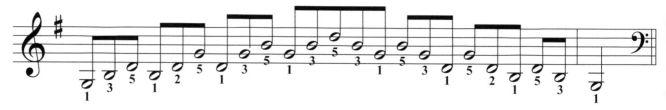

Broken Chords

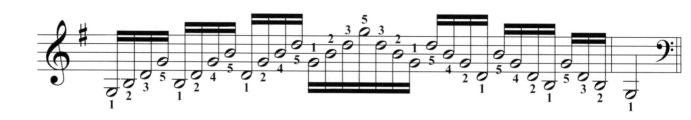

Stephen van der Hoek

D major

Triads

Broken Chords

A major

Triads

Broken Chords

Broken Chords

F major

Triads

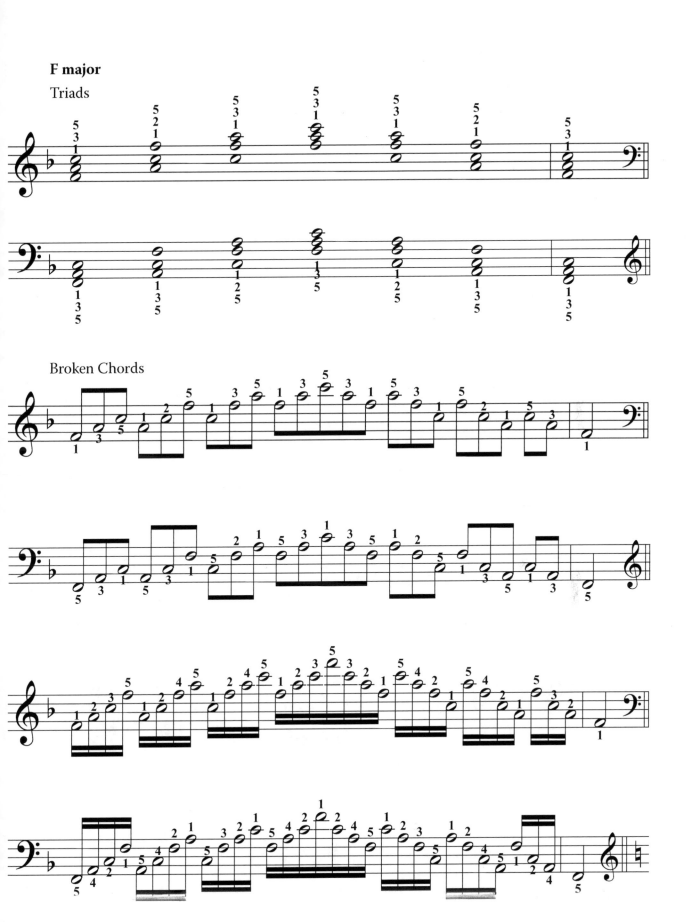

Broken Chords

A minor

Triads

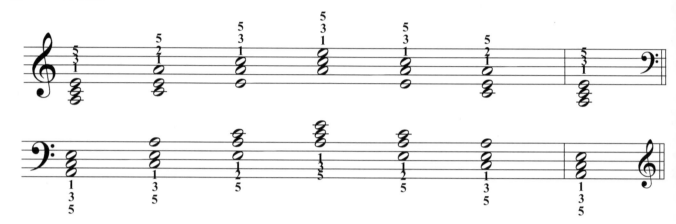

Broken Chords

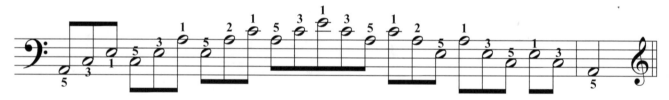

Broken Chords

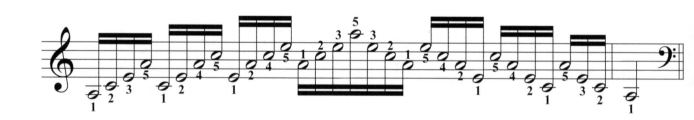

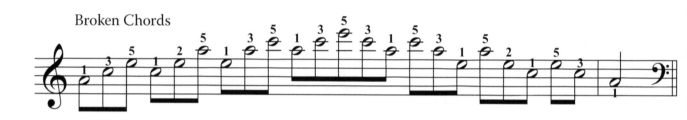

Stephen van der Hoek

E minor

Triads

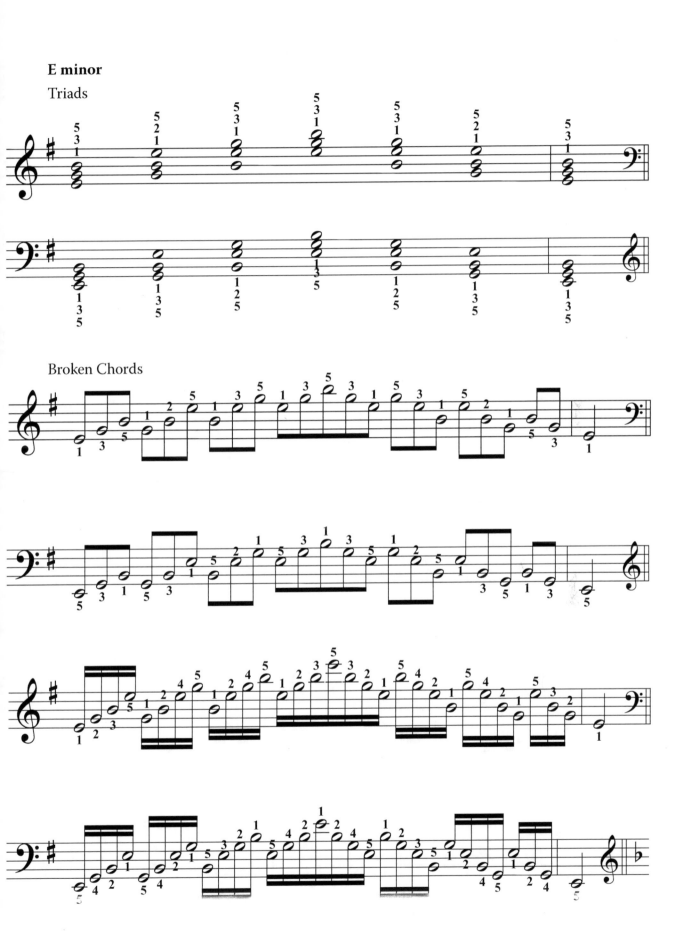

Broken Chords

D minor

Triads

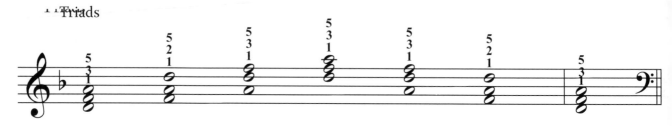

Broken Chords

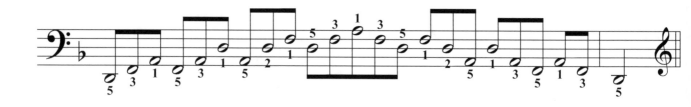

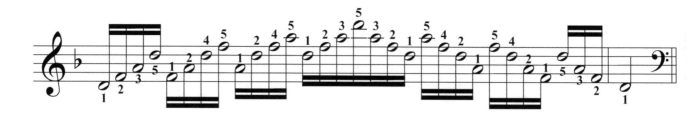

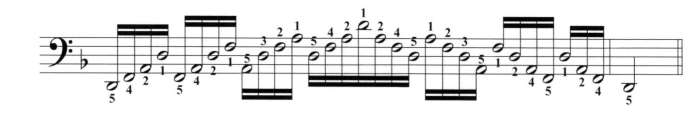

Stephen van der Hoek

Appendix

MELODIC MINOR SCALES

A melodic minor

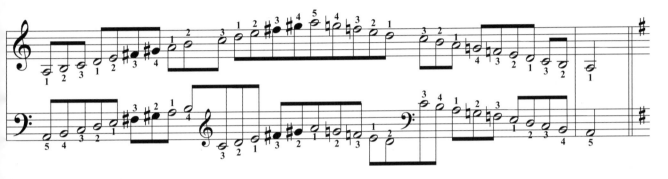

E melodic minor

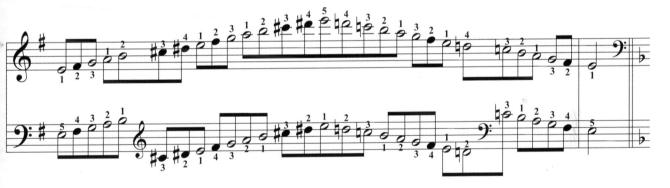

D melodic minor

Printed in the United States
By Bookmasters